CONTENTS

FOREWORD

The African and Caribbean Elders in Scotland (ACES) started in 2019 just before the Covid-19 pandemic and so far has existed mainly on Zoom. ACES is for people aged 60 and above, a friendly group where African and Caribbean elders living in Scotland could come together to celebrate shared cultural heritage and create a space of support, belonging and friendship.

One Life, Two Cultures is a collection of experiences - both good and bad - of African and Caribbean Scots over the past 50 years. It establishes African and Caribbean peoples' experiences as integral to Scottish and wider European society, bringing their voices to the forefront as the stories are told in their own words. These are the stories of real people; their lives are both ordinary and extraordinary at the same time. Their experiences are funny, sad, compelling, and relatable. Documenting these stories helps us to understand the richness and cultural diversity of our communities, while ensuring that these memories are not lost, but passed onto the next generation.

One Life, Two Cultures was developed with the Scottish Civic Trust and supported by a European Heritage Days Stories grant from the Council of Europe and the European Commission, as well as the Year of Stories 2022 Community Stories Fund, which is delivered in partnership between VisitScotland and Museums Galleries Scotland with support from National Lottery Heritage Fund.

Dr Jennifer Novotny, Scottish Civic Trust

Published by African and Caribbean Elders in Scotland CIC

The moral right of the authors has been asserted.

Images courtesy of ACES.

Text Copyright © 2023 by African & Caribbean Elders in Scotland (ACES)

British Library Cataloguing in Publication Data: A catalogue record for this book is available from the British Library.

ISBN: 978-1-3999-6139-4

Cover design by Christian Noelle Charles

Editor: Mary Osei-Oppong

Proofreader(s): Mary Osei-Oppong

Layout and design by The Evolve Group

Patricia Iredia, Ph.D.

MY LIFE STORY

Patricia Iredia, Ph.D.

MY LIFE STORY

I am originally from Nigeria. My first experience of the UK was when I was a twenty year old undergraduate in Nigeria, in 1975. I came over with my mates during the summer holidays to work in London. Life then was very carefree as we were only here for three months and spent all the time doing casual work through Recruitment Agencies. I worked in the post office at Kings Cross London, serving drinks and selling snacks as well as cleaning up after the workers' break time.

I came to live permanently in the UK in 1980, just after I got married to Isaac Iredia, we lived in Belfast, and he was a trainee doctor then. We moved to Scotland and lived in Stornoway, Isle of Lewis in 1996 after he secured a job as a consultant gynaecologist there. In Nigeria, I worked as a civil servant with the Department of Education.

I met my husband at his sister's wedding and eighteen months later I came to Belfast to join my husband. I studied for a postgraduate diploma in Education at Queen's University before I had my first two children. I later had one child in Wales and two in London.

At some point, we were thinking of relocating back to Nigeria, so he accepted a job in Saudi Arabia and the children and I went back to Nigeria but spent all holidays in Saudi Arabia. We moved back to the UK in 1996 when he got a job in Stornoway, Lewis, Western Isles, Scotland. After eight years there, he died of cancer. I was left with the last two children at home for another three years until they started university and we relocated to Glasgow in 2007.

Stornoway was different, an island. On our arrival, we found it exciting because it was a novelty and I thought "Oh my God, this is the end

of the earth!" but it felt like home; all the neighbours were very friendly, in and out of each other's house. We did not lock our doors; there was no need for a key - I had one key to the front door for eleven years and was not scared that anyone would burgle or cause us any harm.

We experienced the occasional racism from kids by name calling but it was the adult ones that stunned us. At the school's prize-giving event, any achievement / participation by the pupils was usually acknowledged and medals were awarded.

On one occasion, two of my children won a national competition for the school in Art and Storytelling, so, we kept waiting for it to be announced, then the MC announced that the head teacher had just returned from Edinburgh with "some children" who won "some competition." To this day it wrenches my heart when I remember how the children reacted.

My family was stunned as my children's names were not mentioned, and my son said with tears in his eyes," "Dad I am sorry that I didn't get any medal." My husband called the headteacher the next day to complain and he said, "My children have names, and it is a shame that children who brought honour to the school were not acknowledged." She was very apologetic and came back to the house with medals.

In secondary school, there were instances where the children were asked "did you do this assignment by yourself or did your dad work on it for you?" This wrong assumption that Black children cannot produce high-standard work could lead to their work being marked down, and that is the ugly face of racism, thankfully, not every teacher was like that.

I would say, overall, my children growing up in Stornoway was a positive experience for all of them. There were more positive than negative because they were the only Black children in the school. They got a lot of support from the school, and they prevailed, and they all did very well. I can proudly say, three of them are doctors, and two are nurses, with nine first degrees between them. All my children; four daughters and one son are married.

I was a full-time homemaker and volunteered with the school library. After the death of my husband, I volunteered with the Council Day Care Centre. The boss saw me one day and said, "why don't you go and work in the home with adults with learning disabilities, it's near your house," so that was how I started and worked there for almost three years as a relief Social Care Worker.

When I first moved to Glasgow in 2007, I was very unsettled and spent more than half of every year in Nigeria for the first few years. The idea was to go back to Nigeria for good.

I soon changed my mind and brought the itinerant lifestyle to a halt and finally settled in Glasgow! I have been self-employed with some online and property businesses, but it was so lonely that I wanted human contact apart from family – my children were at university and when they came back home, laptop and phone dominated and we would talk on the phone in the same house!

I joined the African Caribbean Women Association (ACWA) Scotland to meet other African women and made new friends. I was elected as the Chairperson after nine years of being in ACWA and stayed as a Chair for four years. I volunteer with various organisations. I am currently the treasurer of the Glasgow Women Voluntary Sector Network, a Forum member of Scottish Minority Older People, and a Panel Member of Children's Hearing, Scotland.

I am active in my widows' and widowers' social group, my writing group, and my church group. I am an amateur writer and an aspiring author. I have ten grandchildren from my children who keep me on my toes. I help my children with childcare, especially in emergencies, which happen quite often!

I joined the African and Caribbean Elders group at its inception, just before Covid-19 struck. Lockdown showed us the need for friendship and connectedness, and I am most pleased that African Caribbean Elders were up to the challenge of providing a staunch support group for all the members throughout the pandemic and beyond. Long Live ACES!

David Olwa

DETERMINED TO SUCCEED

David Olwa

DETERMINED TO SUCCEED

Originally, I am from a region in Northern Uganda and I now live in Linlithgow Royal Burgh in West Lothian in Scotland.

I came to Britain on 20th March 1969 and stayed for a short time in London. My next stop was Newcastle-upon-Tyne, then I made my big move to Scotland. I was told that Scottish people were friendly, so I said let me come and witness it for myself.

I came to Britain as a qualified Medical Assistant, a qualification not well-recognised in the United Kingdom. I needed to retrain as a Medical Assistant in the UK so when in Newcastle-upon-Tyne I decided to retrain. I passed my exams at the Royal Edinburgh Hospital, the University Hospital.

Coming to Scotland, I was told Scottish people were strict, so I expected that being a small country, life would be a little better than in England and that I would be able to integrate well into Scottish society.

I was well received on my arrival in Scotland in 1970, the year Edinburgh hosted its first Commonwealth Games. The games highlighted the spirit of the Scottish people's kindness and friendliness towards visitors, which helped me to join in the celebrations it started my integration.

I was given a place after I finished the training, working in the hospital also, I was given accommodation in a place called Bo'ness. It was a typical miners' village, at the time it seems to me that the residents in Bo'ness had not seen black people before, so it was a big challenge for me to know how I was going to be accepted in the community. They all knew each other, I decided to join the football team in Bo'ness to help me get friendly with the local communities.

I spoke to the manager about my willingness to train with his team, I told him jokingly that now that you have allowed me to join the team, the team is going to win the cup and that was in 1975. Bo'ness United had never won the cup in 30 years. When I joined, we played and Bo'ness United won the cup for the first time.

In celebration, I sat the cup on my head to show how joyous I was, and I became known to the local communities. I remember people were saying "oh wow, wow". Wherever I went, I heard happy football fans cheering "David, David". I knew I had pulled a good act because I thought it was going to be difficult. I was not going to be accepted and thankfully I became part of the community.

The job situation was very tricky. I was overly qualified for the job I was doing but because of fear and I think racism, I remained calm. I noticed the behaviours of my colleagues, knowing I could not be given a senior position. I remember being told, "oh, you are highly qualified, have you ever thought of going to Uganda to get a good job?" They asked that question not realising that was racism. I would usually respond, I'm trained in Britain, I've got the British standard, why would you think my qualification will only be good in Uganda and not here? Oh no, we didn't mean it that way, so what do you mean?"

They feared that when you put David to be the senior man of the job, how would the people react? It was the generality of the senior colleague, and it never occurred to them that was racism.

As a couple, my late wife and I were walking to Falkirk for shopping when we met some young lads. They were known as Skinheads. The boys were notorious and were verbally abusive to us on the street. My wife expected me to respond to their abusive behaviours, but I remained calm because I was once trained in how to deal with such situations.

I wanted my wife and me to get to a place of safety before contacting the police. At this point, a CID officer who has been observing our movements made himself known and informed us that he had witnessed what happened and he was going to contact the police to report the incident himself. Police arrived at the scene and arrested the boys. This

showed that there was racism in the community.

The Police Superintendent who received the report wrote to us apologising for what happened. I still have the letter and it was the first time I experienced change. I wondered what impression Scotland would have made if this had happened to an African dignitary on a visit.

At my wife's place of work, she was discriminated against. There was what they called grading in nursing - clinical grading. My wife noticed most of her white colleagues were given higher grades except herself and other black nurses irrespective of their qualifications.

She raised this as an issue and complained to the health board, and it led to a court case that lasted fourteen years. Can you imagine? It was difficult to fight big organisations like the health board. They were interested in protecting their name. The worker's union couldn't help either and that was when I realised fighting racism was difficult.

Even in 2022, we are still fighting racism. This is the Scotland that I was told was very friendly.

As a result of all these experiences, I joined the union – Unison - and in the end, I started the black section/unit of the health board – Lothian Health Board and it's still active. I have retired now, but that unit is still there because I know black African people are still struggling with racism.

Through the union, I was engaged in providing proper education on racism to fight the problem. At times the racism training was delivered to parents for this message to filter through to young people. We thought this could help raise awareness of racism in society and possibly reduce the problem of workplace discrimination.

Messages like 'Give Racism a Red Card', are simply fire-fighting and won't solve problems of racism. The issue needs to be addressed from its root cause.

At the time, Glasgow had more black people in their community than Edinburgh. And there was less support from black people for fear of losing their jobs and other consequences if they were seen as supporting our initiative.

However, our messages from the union's black unit were directed to the larger ethnic minority community, including the Chinese, Pakistanis, Arabs and Filipinos, many of whom were coming into the country at the time as nurses with less understanding of the English language.

Other ethnic minorities joined the unit when they realised our activities were not about colour, but rather the interests of the ethnic community.

During my union activities, I moved home a few times. But primarily attending events and conferences across Scotland, some of which I was challenging the STUC. It was a standing ovation for me at one of such conferences in Glasgow, where I made it known to the attendees that Africans are not inferior.

Around this time, I received a message that a professor at a University was working to publish a book in which he was to claim that black people are inferior. This academic work of his led some students of the university going on to protest, eventually, the professor was dismissed from the university and the book was never published.

Professor Sir Geoff Palmer and I also challenged one American scholar with a publication of a similar derogatory idea – that black people are inferior – because we considered the word racist.

I knew the fight against racism may take longer, but I determined not to give up the fight. To give up would have been a loss. I strongly believe that educating children together with their parents and teachers and then the wider community on racism, and then introducing to them the message that all people are human beings and are the same, no matter the colour of their skin.

What had happened in history is gone and should not define anyone, any longer. The previous events should be addressed as history. As such, the act of taking down statues will not solve the problems, rather these statues should be considered part of history. The effort of people who are alive is not to repeat history, but rather do better.

I always want to have the opportunity to talk to more people about racism. I never felt the need to give up. I believe with the effort of everyone, soon everyone will come together with a united aim and understanding that irrespective of skin colour and other characteristics, we are all the same, we are all human beings.

The verdict we got in my wife's racism court case against her employer was not what we expected. In the court case, we lacked good support from our black community, as they were all scared to attend the tribunal. Most of her colleagues who were giving evidence were also scared, as it was a case of racism. We realised it was very difficult to get support when we were in the tribunal.

Although my wife won her case at the first ruling, the health board appealed the case as they were out to protect their name. The outcome in the end protected the name of the health board. I considered this institutionalised racism.

I think my wife and I said: 'we do not want this to happen to any other black people.' This was the major reason for her determination on the case.

She wanted to gain protection for black people against discrimination during their careers, especially where they have the necessary qualifications for job progression. I had wished to write a book on this experience, but sadly my wife passed away three years ago.

In tribute, her colleagues referred to her as a star, respectful, who was well experienced and professional in her role. These colleagues gave several anecdotes.

For what we both did, we were invited to the Royal Garden Party in Edinburgh. Dignitaries at the event assumed I was an ambassador. The organiser offered us a chance to meet with Princess Anne, who shared with my wife activities of a children's hospital and a home in Nairobi, Kenya where she was a patron.

Her chat with my wife lasted over ten minutes compared to the 2-3 minutes she had with other people. 'Children' was such a common factor between Princess Anne and my wife during their conversation, it was this that made the Princess chat with my wife longer.

My planned book would highlight the role and contributions black and African people have offered to Scottish society. We are educated and we have made contributions to our society. We paid taxes like anybody else and we want to be equal because we are all human beings.

I miss my wife. Her friends who are from all over the world also miss her. At our wedding, we had three bridesmaids who were from Ghana, Kenya, and Mauritius. Our wedding was at the Royal Barra. Though I am Ugandan, I recently returned from Kenya, where she was from, to put a headstone and had a thanksgiving in her memory. I had a similar memorial for her too in Uganda.

A charity organisation I started drilled water in a poor area and this is still supplying water to the community. The people of this community say to me now: "we have water because of Dorothy and you".

We also helped get hospital and medical equipment donations to a big hospital in Uganda, where the church we built is located. Because of all these contributions and activities, several people, including family members miss Dorothy, not just myself.

In Linlithgow, here in Scotland, people including children say to me whenever I take a walk alone: "David, where is your wife today". And I do reply to them "she's somewhere".

I miss her, but that is life, part of life! Those who believe in God say: "God has called her". Although nobody knows. They say, "she's in a safe place". We don't know, but she's not here.

Personally and generally, I feel I have achieved the understanding because if I didn't come to the UK and just lived in Africa without the UK experience, I would not have known that we have been brainwashed. I would not have learnt about racism. I would not have learnt how the Western world and its society operate.

I have achieved a lot because I have gained knowledge which had given me the opportunity to offer my service to Uganda. Although I was already trained in the health service in Uganda and I continued here, where I enhanced my knowledge.

Through an arrangement with a Member of Parliament, I received training in the Parliament. This afforded me the opportunity to start a project on developing a unit of health service planning that would be working in the President's office in Uganda. I had the chance together with five seconded civil servants to set up a new era in planning health service and policy. But before we could do that, the government in Uganda was overthrown by the army, so I could not deliver this project. All the hard work could have helped the Uganda people but it was not meant to be.

Generally, my achievement would be, getting the experiences which, I would not have got by remaining in Uganda. These experiences came from the fact that I studied and live in our society here in Scotland. This engagement with society gave me a good understanding of the people, their values, and their culture. The engagements made me different from people who came before me to study for two to three years and return to their various countries.

My main achievements, I started the black section of Unison; I started the retired member of Unison, which is still active and I was the chair; I started a charity organisation which has continued to provide help to people.

Quite many other achievements, which I can't count. I couldn't have done them if I didn't come to this country. Although, perseverance and determination played a major part in gaining achievements. People who were abusive to me because of my activities, returned to me to express apologies after realising the impact of my efforts. But you know you cannot judge a book by its cover.

I was trained in health service, as Medical Assistant, you were trained like a doctor. An initiative of our government then was to provide us with further training to enable us to convert to full medical doctors, so that as doctors we can fill the gap in the health system. But politicians wanted us to fill roles in dispensaries instead. I did not like this idea.

As the Medical Assistant job was not recognised in the medical profession internationally, I was not satisfied with this role. I was in the role briefly, working professionally and with many people including white people. So, when I had the opportunity to come to Britain, I contacted British Council who then arranged for someone to receive me at the airport on arrival. In London, I was received by a white man with the name card 'David Olwa' waiting for me at the airport.

I was offered more privileges during the flight, including an opportunity to meet with pilots in the cockpit.

On arrival, my career experience and education were recognised in the UK. All the courses I took were short courses because of my qualifications from Uganda. Then Makerere University Uganda was the same standard as Oxford, Cambridge and the University of Edinburgh. Then as well, all the lecturers were from the UK, so our qualifications were recognised. That was the advantage because we indeed had proper training in Uganda.

The attitude from people and society that: "why do they come to take our jobs", which is racism needs to be corrected by stating the roles and contributions of black people to the healthcare system, environment and the community.

A Scottish chap once said to me: "David, tell me why I should promote you and not promote a Scottish person?". I told him: 'you are being racist because I am a better-qualified person than the white person and you are discriminating against me'.

With my remark, which highlights the implication of his statement, the chap could only retort: "I was just asking". This to me was his way of excusing his attitude towards my race.

The wider Scottish society and indeed the United Kingdom is not well informed of the contributions of black people in this country. This ACES book must help to educate the people of the United Kingdom about the need to show respect and recognition to black people who are here. They have always been receiving acceptance and huge respect from Africans whenever they visit any part of Africa.

People of this country through this book should understand and know that the black community are playing their part to contribute to the development of the UK. From different aspects of life – education, health, retail, entrepreneurship and others. Black people have made and are making good contributions to Scottish society. We have done it!

Right now, Mukami McCrum MBE and I, are involved in a group in West Lothian about slavery – the legacy of slavery. We are of the view that the image of slavery is still part of the perception of white society to black people in our community. We hope to develop a report that would be available in schools for children to have access to correct this perception.

Dr Harriette Campbell

A RAY OF SUNSHINE

Dr Harriette Campbell

A RAY OF SUNSHINE

At 77 years old, I am an activist, a founding member of the African and Caribbean Women's Association (ACWA) in Scotland in 1988, along with other women's groups and organisations, including African and Caribbean Elders in Scotland (ACES). I am also a mother of two beautiful grown-up girls and two adorable teenage grandchildren.

I was born on 7th October 1944 in Bathurst, now Banjul, in The Gambia, which was then a British Colony. I think about what was happening during those months leading to my birth. My parents must have been very happy.

I am the eldest of 7 siblings (two girls and five boys) and was educated in primary and secondary schools mainly run by missionaries. I was inspired by my mum who was a nurse, so after leaving school I embarked on working in the nursing profession.

I wanted to make my mum happy, as she wanted me to follow in her footsteps. I trained in the Royal Victoria Hospital in The Gambia and became a certificated Nurse Midwife. It was a rewarding career. During my eight years of working, I delivered numerous babies in hospitals and home deliveries before rendering my resignation.

In August 1970 I relocated to the United Kingdom to continue my nursing career. My journey took me a day and a half by aeroplane. (The alternative would have been by boat, which then took seven days.) This was my maiden flight from home, with an overnight stop in Las Palmas before my destination in the UK. The airport was massively different from the one I left behind.

Arriving in the UK was a culture shock. The weather was very cold, people were very serious, the sun did not shine, and the buildings were all so different from back home. My friend's husband met me at the airport. I was very sick throughout our journey in the car (one of the reasons why I did not learn to drive at home).

The streets were not paved with gold! (laughs). Finally, after a very long journey, we arrived at the family home in Calne, a town in Wiltshire, England. I was warmly welcomed. This was a brief stop for two weeks and I managed to shop for warm clothes. I reported at the Nurses' Home and was welcomed by the House Matron and a few nurses. On my first night at the Nurses' Home, I cried all night. I was twenty-five years old and homesick.

I quickly made friends. The home was a massive building, which accommodated nurses from different parts of the world. We travelled to work in coaches together and ate together. The food was different - there were limited African products, but we improvised. There was plenty of fun and laughter.

At the beginning of my nursing career in the UK, patients made me feel uncomfortable. As a nurse, I continued to show patience, especially when the patients told me not to touch them, go back to where I came from, and go and have a wash because they assumed that I was dirty.

A few of us nurses travelled together after our exams to Austria. It was an exciting holiday and we visited the famous castle where Chitty, Chitty, Bang, Bang was filmed. We hired bikes daily and had fun.

I moved to Glasgow, Scotland, in 1973. I remembered my Scottish teachers, who taught me about the lochs and lakes, Scottish country dancing and the reel. What made me choose Scotland? My nosiness. I wanted to know more about Scottish people, but I was disappointed about some people's attitude towards me, because of my skin colour.

I was afraid to walk alone in the streets at night, especially in the area where the Nurses' Home was located, which was a deprived and dilapidated area. There was name-calling and stone-throwing.

When I started working in the hospital wards, although, I spoke English, I found it difficult to communicate. Depending on where you are in the city, you are referred to as "hen". My reply was that "I was a chicken," just for a laugh.

Another common word, when a patient was asked to do something and could not do it, is the reply "I canny". To me, this word meant "hot pepper" not "I cannot"! Gradually I got to understand how culturally diverse Scottish people are, depending on what geographical area you live in.

I have memories of sitting and talking to patients who felt alone. I tried

cheering them up. I was even given the nickname "Sunshine" whenever I entered this medical ward. I asked why and was told that I am always smiling and just a ray of sunshine.

For the last 15 years of my career, I worked in the Acute Stroke Unit, a specialist unit for stroke patients from all age groups. Seeing the recovery of most patients and

their relatives' smiles and laughter made me feel happy to be part of the journey.

At 56 years old I decided to be trained as a counsellor and I received my Diploma in Cognitive Behavioural Therapy (with support from a couple of the ward consultants). My experience helped my mum's recovery when she suffered her stroke at the age of 84. I retired at the age of 60 in 2004.

A colleague and I working as nurses noticed that there was a gap in the National Health Service in Scotland for awareness and treatment for Sickle Cell and Thalassaemia, inherited red blood cell disorders. African and Caribbean communities are mainly affected.

We started our awareness-raising campaign by organising conferences and seminars, engaging with policymakers and the communities. This earned me an Honorary Doctorate Degree, from Glasgow Caledonian University in July 2021, which I accepted with pride and great honour. I am now an Honourary Doctor of Science.

Emelia Agbotta

MAKING A DIFFERENCE

Emelia Agbotta

MAKING A DIFFERENCE

I was born and brought up in Ghana, West Africa. I have three grown-up children and two lovely grandsons. My reasons for coming to the UK were to update my knowledge and upgrade my skills. I pursued a B.Sc. Nursing Studies and M.Sc. Advanced Health Studies at Paisley University and Strathclyde University run by Bell College Hamilton campus.

I arrived in Glasgow on the 27th of November 2001, on a cold, rainy winter morning. I was taken from the airport to Wyndford Locks Nursing Home at Maryhill where I started my adaptation. Work started the following day. I had orientation, and I was given the company policy to sign. I wasn't given a chance to read through the document, I was told to sign here and there. It felt so unusual. Who was I to ask questions?

Fortunately, there were some African healthcare professionals also working there, so they helped me to get around and know what I was doing. As soon as I had my PIN, I started looking for a job in a hospital because I was not used to working in a nursing home and was not comfortable as I didn't have a critical care nursing background.

My nursing career began in Ghana where I obtained my state registered nurse status, state midwifery and Advanced Diploma in Critical Nursing. I practiced nursing for several years before coming to the UK. My first NHS job was at Victoria Infirmary, where I worked in a medical ward.

The ward manager was so lovely and nice to work with. The challenge I had on that ward was from a male nurse who was racial and discriminative towards me, so much so that I even wanted to go back to Ghana, but my faith and belief system saw me through.

Compared to Ghana, the cold in Glasgow is very severe from December to March. In Ghana, we don't have snow, so there is no need for special footwear, but here in Glasgow, you need winter boots. What I had was not the right type of footwear. A rubber sole footwear that has slip resistance was needed to walk on the snow and since mine didn't have that feature, I kept falling whenever it snowed. My fingers and toes were

often numb due to the extremely cold weather. I discussed this with my Brazilian colleague, she took me shopping to purchase the appropriate winter clothes and shoes.

It wasn't easy at all. The interaction with some staff members in the hospital was challenging. There was discrimination everywhere. I had to fight for my rights. Even when I was the one in charge of the ward; some of the staff did not show me respect, because I came from Ghana with African heritage. Their attitude to me was abhorrent.

Action speaks louder than words, their behaviour and attitude towards me were self-explanatory. "Who is she for me to take orders from?" They would ask. I stood my ground and did not give in and got on with my work. The worst was when the auxiliary nurses and families kept constantly asking, "Are you in charge?"

I remember the day when one of the auxiliary nurses came to work and found out that I was in charge, she left. She couldn't work with me as her line manager. I reported this as the reason she left, but nothing was done about it.

I had a lot of gifts and thank you cards from patients and their relatives which I thought was very kind of them but some of my colleagues were not happy about these acknowledgments. I did the best for the patients in my care. Furthermore, I saw nursing as a calling, not a vocation. So, I practiced it with all my body and soul. Waking up early in the morning wasn't easy, especially during the winter months when work started at quarter past seven.

I never saw daylight. I left for work in darkness and returned home in darkness. During summer, seeing the blue sky always lifted my spirit, and that too didn't last long. There was a lot of prejudice from other colleagues too, but I dealt with it.

I remember while attending to an older lady, she said, "black, black, black sheep, what are you doing in my country? Go to your country!!!" I was upset and said to her, "I am here to help with the health delivery because the NHS found the need to recruit from abroad as there was a shortage."

Also, as usual, when the United Kingdom needed help for people to go to war, they called on Commonwealth countries to help, that's why I am here. Besides, I will not take a plot of land to Ghana the day I leave the UK. The patient next to her witnessed what was going on and told her to acknowledge how upset I was, she repeated, "but she is a black, black, girl."

The Scottish accent was difficult to understand to start with. People will be talking to me, I kept saying 'pardon' or, "can you repeat please?" Some people were rude to the point of asking, "Who employed you at all? How did you get a job here when you don't understand anything?" However, in time I was able to understand the accent and was able to communicate effectively.

I went through so many challenges; some I have forgotten and others will always remain with me. Discrimination and racism are like incurable cancer and no medication can provide effective treatment.

The pursuit of my first degree went very well, all the lectures were lovely and helpful. But with my second degree, I felt I was in the wrong place. Two of the lecturers, one male and one female who shared the same office, made my life unbearable. They were discriminatory and racist towards me.

The female lecturer threw my essay at me, saying, "There is something in the essay." The male lecturer gave the class guidance notes and as I was leaving the classroom, he took mine back but allowed others to leave with theirs. I pleaded and said to him I will return it the next lecture day, but he refused. He said to me I wasn't supposed to take it home and I was supposed to leave it in class. I was the only African in the class.

It rains a lot in Glasgow, the cold, the wind, and as well as snow. I have always said the three together made me miss Ghana. We've got sun for twelve hours even though it can rain heavily during the rainy season, it is nowhere near as cold as Glasgow.

The food was another problem, I had to travel from Glasgow every two months to London to get African foodstuffs. Despite this, I became used to the local Scottish food after a while.

I have a Christian background. Going to church and worshipping God was part of my family tradition. I went to a church and I was not well received, so I found another one near George Square where a lot of Africans worship, and they were lovely.

The pastor phoned me on a Wednesday, just three days after my first visit, I felt welcome and fell in love with the church and the congregation. The church is caring and accepting, so I had been attending since my first visit. I have made a lot of friends within the church.

I found a lot of cultural differences, especially in communication with older people. In Ghana, when an older person is speaking to you, you don't talk back or argue with them. Here you see children talking back to their parents and people not showing any respect, calling them by their first name, it is so different from my cultural background.

I like Glasgow's green environment, it is like where I come from in Africa, very green. Interesting places to visit. But the discrimination and racism make me sad and feel excluded from the society I live in and am part of.

Also, I kept telling myself, "It is God who made me." I don't come from a different planet, but all living beings are from the same planet. What my future will be is in the hands of God. I didn't go to the creator and asked to be made a Ghanaian or African. I'm proud of who I am and my heritage.

As a Ghanaian in a foreign country, I found it necessary to join the Ghana Welfare Association West of Scotland and served as a financial secretary for two terms. Also, I am a member of the Scotland - Ghana friendship society which is made up of Scottish who once lived and worked in Ghana and some Ghanaians also living in Scotland.

Since I love charity work and interacting with people from all over the world I joined the African Caribbean Women Association (ACWA) Scotland and the African and Caribbean Elders in Scotland (ACES) during the Covid-19 pandemic.

I have a passion for working with communities, I am the chairperson for Tropika life support Scotland and proud of that. A charity that deals with educating the minority by organising health talks, forums and discussions on health issues.

My holidays back in Ghana are also full of activities. I have participated in updating skills and upgrading the knowledge of the nurses as well as teaching CPR and first aid. Finally, a member of the Ghana International Nurses Welfare Association with its leadership in the UK. I have enjoyed working in the UK and in Ghana.

I still work at Queen Elizabeth University Hospital. The change was so drastic that many of my colleagues left. In the old hospital, we were like a family, but the new hospital feels too big. I am not interested in just moaning about prejudice but challenging it to bring about a change is important to me and how I can influence to make a difference.

Esther Solaja (nee Babalola)

I ENJOY LIVING IN SCOTLAND

Esther Solaja (nee Babalola)

I ENJOY LIVING IN SCOTLAND

I was born in Lagos State, Nigeria. I studied a secretarial course after my secondary education at the age of 18 and worked for 6 years as a secretary. While on holiday in the UK I met my future husband, Kayode Solaja in Glasgow in 1986.

Our relationship started with three years of long-distance communication which wasn't easy at that time, there was no mobile phone, our only means of communication was by letters, which took three to four weeks to be received and the reply also took about the same length of time. I returned to the UK in 1989 and we got married in the same year. We had three wonderful and independent children.

My first job in Glasgow was as an auxiliary nurse at Stobhill Hospital. I also worked in several private nursing homes. I worked in the nursing field for ten years before I decided to go to university to do a nursing degree. I studied for two years before illness prevented me from completing the course.

When I got better, I went on to study Childcare and Education at Reid Keir College in Paisley. It was a two-year course and I had to be contented with some people refusing to sit next to me or work with me because of my skin colour. After completing the course, I secured a job and worked as a nursery nurse in a private nursery school in Bridge of Weir.

Also, I did voluntary work for two years in Paisley, working with young people with additional support needs before we move to Dumfries. In Dumfries, I worked for one and half years at Activities Resource Centre for eighteen to twenty-five-year-olds, as a Learning Assistant.

The worst racism I experienced occurred when I worked with a computer company in Paisley as a catering assistant at weekends in the 90s. About six months into

the job the manager informed me that a complaint had been made against me that there was an unusual smell whenever I was around.

I could not believe what he told me; in response, I told him that maybe the people that made the complaint were the ones that smell because I always bathed or showered every day, so how could I smell? I left the company because of that.

When my family moved to Dumfries in 2001, I worked with Dumfries and Galloway Council for fourteen years either as a nursery nurse or support for learning assistant in the local schools. Colleagues were pleasant, including the managers and I am still friends with some of them even after retiring.

Two years before I took early retirement in 2016, I was transferred to a special needs school and the manager did not want me to work with the children; I was only allowed to do odd jobs. I felt I was being discriminated against, my experience in this school was not a good one and I ended up taking early retirement.

In my leisure time, I like to read, knit, cook, exercise and do some gardening. Also, I enjoy socialising locally and within the UK, with other members of Dumfries Get Together, which I joined in 2012. I started playing bowling in 2014 with other members of the Dumfries Bowling Club and playing competitively with other clubs. Apart from racism and discrimination, I enjoy living in Scotland; it offers so many opportunities as well as within the UK.

Fatou Cham Gitteh

EDUCATION IS KEY

Fatou Cham Gitteh

EDUCATION IS KEY

I visited Scotland a couple of times, I discovered that Scottish people were friendly, so I decided to move to Scotland in 2014. I travelled from The Gambia in 2005 and settled in Birmingham before moving to Scotland and I have lived here in Glasgow for eight years now.

I have a family friend in Glasgow and each time she visited me in Birmingham, she encouraged me to move to Scotland. We exchanged family party invitations whenever we had a celebration in our different cities. I moved to Scotland and truly, I have no regrets.

My friend in Glasgow looked happy and led a better life. Also, I noticed that there was a lesser crime rate in Glasgow compared to Birmingham and these formed my expectations to move to Scotland.

When I moved to Glasgow, I accompanied my friends to visit community charities and food banks. Some places were welcoming and others were not. So, I stopped going to these places. At one point in college, I felt discriminated against.

During my first year in college, I was usually the first person to arrive in the morning due to the bus timetable in my area. The bus arrived at my bus stop every 30 minutes and this meant I must leave home early so I don't arrive late to college.

I noticed some of my classmates would not sit next to me, they sat on other empty chairs whilst the seat close to me remained empty. I had a Nigerian classmate who usually came and sat next to me, this made me feel better. I felt unwelcome among others and discriminated against.

Even during the group activities in class, my classmates did not want me to join their groups except when the teacher instructed them to include me in their group. I had different challenges, though, you'd always find good people and bad people anywhere.

My flatmate and I had an experience trying to get on a bus with some teenage boys hurling abusive words at us saying "You asylum seekers, go back to your f**king country!" It seems to them that, any black person they saw was an asylum seeker. The boys' behaviour stopped us from boarding the bus on that day. This experience made me afraid of going out at night.

When I came to Glasgow, there were not many black people as we have today. I looked for where I could find African communities and I was introduced to a man who directed me to where I could find the Gambian community in Glasgow. Although, there were not as many African groups at the time.

When I became part of the Gambian community group, I was invited to the meetings. From there on, I started to attend other events and it was in one of the workshops I met a woman who from her outfit, I could tell she was a Gambian and she is called Harriette Campbell. I walked up to her to introduce myself and in our conversation, I realised she is from the Gambia.

Coincidentally, I discovered her mother was a nurse in the hospital I was born. When I relayed Harriette's story to my mum over the phone to her in The Gambia, my mum said she remembers Harriette's mum, a nurse in our community.

Harriette introduced me to the African Caribbean Women's Association (ACWA) Scotland and I have been a member of the Association ever since.

I live in Springburn, I know many people now and have made friends within the community. We all know each other, and we enjoy each other's company, because of these friendships, most of the time, I am not lonely or homesick.

Also, technology has made communication with my family in the Gambia easily accessible, especially with internet calls using WhatsApp. I call my children whenever I want to mostly on video calls. This method of communication has made things better since their dad passed away.

I still miss home at times during festivities and family celebrations because I know it would be different if I was there in The Gambia. For example, I have missed my son's traditional wedding and missed performing my traditional rites of receiving the bride when she is brought to her husband's family. It was heartbreaking for me to hear my son saying "I need my mum" in the traditional wedding video. Thankfully, my sisters were there to take my place and performed the rites on my behalf.

On my son's wedding day, Marion my Scottish friend decided to take me, her husband and my Iranian friend out for the whole day. She took me out to Loch Lomond to cheer me up for not being able to attend my son's memorable day.

My biggest achievement had been furthering my education and gaining access to go to college in Scotland. I have achieved a lot in coming to

Scotland. I have been able to get good grades in most of my exams. I have gained a lot of qualifications through studies that would enable me to secure a better job in the future and earn a good income.

I can work as a care worker, in community jobs, in support care in the hospital, in mental health and in first aid. During the last COP26 in Glasgow, I put myself forward and became a volunteer First Aider. Feeling like part of the community has really helped me to integrate fully into Scotland.

I have many good friends now and know community groups that are helpful to me and they have made me feel part of them. When I lost my husband, I did not feel isolated or lonely because my friends and groups helped me during the period I was mourning. They stood with me and remained by my side through the trying times and I saw all of these as achievements. Anytime I needed help, I knew where to go to.

In return, I have also made myself available to offer support and give help to others when needed within my community. I had always been there for my friend and her children particularly with their homework when she needs assistance, I have helped new arrivals in Scotland that needed to know new places to explore.

I am also glad that I came to Scotland, I have been able to support my children through school and they have now become graduates. I have also graduated from college. I am glad that we have all been able to get an education. Even if I die today, I would be at peace. I thank God and I know my children can use it as a good legacy because I have shown them footsteps to emulate.

Justina Odom

MY FAMILY IS MY LIFE

Justina Odom

MY FAMILY IS MY LIFE

I arrived at Heathrow Airport, holding a child of mixed heritage, about three months old. This is how the story came to be in July 1963. At Accra Kotoka International Airport in Ghana, I met a couple, a Ghanaian gentleman and his English wife. The gentleman approached me and said to me he was not travelling with his wife and requested that I helped his wife while in transit.

We boarded the plane and not long after the child began to cry. The mother asked me to help her. I took the child, fed her and held her in my arms. The mother passed me the child's feeding bag and innocently I kept the bag and the child until we landed at Heathrow Airport.

Disembarking from the plane, I spotted my husband waving to me and I waved back. He signalled and questioned who the child was. I turned to identify the mother and to my surprise, I saw her disappearing.

I ran after her calling out "Excuse me! Excuse me!" But she never turned to see who was calling. I ran faster hopping to reach her and shouting out "Excuse me again, this is your child". She replied by saying "Oh, thank you" and she took the child and walked on.

I was almost left with a child whom my husband knew nothing about. My husband and friends joked about this bizarre situation. This could have ended up looking like child abduction and the situation could have ruined my career and life as at the time I worked as a typist for customs and excise in Ghana.

The company I worked for dealt with expatriates who came to work in Ghana. I loved my job, but there was a need for me to join my husband in London.

In London, my first job was with a company called Dunset radio factory, they built transmitters and radio grams. On the first day at work, my husband asked me to make some sandwiches for lunch for work. I did not have a suitable lunch box to carry the sandwich, my husband gave me an overnight travel bag to carry two small sandwiches. Humour was his forte.

I never did like this job, so I moved to a clothing factory called Executex. That same year, my husband was given a scholarship by the Ghana Government to study banking, so we moved to Leeds in September 1963. I had always thought of furthering my career in secretarial, however, my husband persuaded me to go down a clothing and textile path, to which I listened. I went to enrol in a course in Clothing Technology.

When we arrived in Leeds, we were directed to a hotel and sometime later we arrived in our new flat. At the hotel, we were offered tea and coffee. I opted for black coffee, bearing in mind, that I had never tried it before. I have never drunk coffee since then. My husband chose tea with milk and sugar, he made a better choice than me.

All changed in 1966 when my husband's scholarship was withdrawn, due to the *coup d'etat* in Ghana. Forcing him to find a way to pay his tuition fees led us back to London due to his job offer with Lloyds Bank.

I also got a job at Marks and Son, an evening-wear clothing enterprise. I enjoyed the working environment and stayed there until my first child was born in 1971. After my daughter was born, I changed jobs but remained in the clothing industry. I got a job with Ellis Bridal, creating wedding dresses and evening gowns.

I will fast forward to 2008, a new adventure began when my youngest granddaughter was born and brought us to the beautiful city of Edinburgh. Here, I have made new friends, enjoying my retirement, watching my three beautiful grandchildren grow and instilling in them the value of self-belief, dignity, respect and how their dreams can be realised.

Kayode Solaja

FROM NIGERIA TO SCOTLAND

Kayode Solaja

FROM NIGERIA TO SCOTLAND

I was born in Nigeria and was raised in Okolomo village, Abeokuta. I loved my childhood. I had fun memories growing up in an idyllic village. By the age of eight, I was weaving baskets and selling them for pocket money before moving to Lagos.

I came to the UK in 1974 at the age of fifteen to join my father, Ayodele Solaja, who came to the UK in the late 1960s with his new wife to complete his education. They lived in Glasgow with a five year old daughter and one year old son when I arrived in the UK. My father was researching for his Ph.D. in Total Technology at Strathclyde University.

I met my father at Heathrow airport in London. The first thing he gave me was his coat because he saw me shivering the weather was cold. The clothes I was wearing were not suitable for the weather condition in the UK. When I left Lagos airport, it was sunny, I carried my lightweight jacket as the weather was too hot. With my father's coat on, I felt more comfortable, because it kept me warm during the train journey to Glasgow.

I was due to start my third year of secondary school education in Lagos, but my father suggested I repeat the second year in Glasgow because of a language barrier. It was a good decision because I found the Scottish dialect difficult to understand and people found my accent difficult as well, I looked forward to the end of the school day so that I could escape from school to relax at home. It took me almost one year to understand the Sottish dialect and adjust to the culture.

I found it surprising when I first came to the UK that black people were not welcome in the society, as white people were warmly welcomed with respect and dignity in Nigeria. Some white people were ignorant and have misguided assumptions that their race was better than others, resulting in prejudice and stereotyping of black people.

For instance, if a black person in England did something wrong many white people assumed that all black people were the same, sadly the media encouraged such views. When there was a famine in Ethiopia in 1984-85 and Band Aid was being organised – they called it Aid for Africa as though the aid was for the whole African continent. Things like that fuel people's prejudice and stereotypes.

Two years after arriving in Glasgow my father completed his Ph.D. and he decided to return to Lagos with the rest of the family to take up a managerial position. Job opportunities were limited for black people in the UK at that time. Initially, I was left behind to sit my O-Level exams the following year. One of my father's friends acted as a guardian until I was eighteen years old, and I continued to live in my parent's flat with two older student lodgers. After the exams, I decided to continue my education in Scotland.

After my O-Level exams, I embarked on an engineering course. After completing the course, I secured a job in the industry sector and worked for ten years before moving on to the social care sector for five years in Glasgow and Linwood's areas working with young homeless people in hostels. I relocated to Dumfries town in 2001 with my family when I secured a job as a secondary school teacher of technical education. I retired in 2019 after 21 years of teaching.

I believe in hard work, keeping fit and volunteering to help others in the community. I started volunteering in 1995 and have worked with four different organisations - I started the current volunteering work over a year ago in 2021 with Children's Hearings Scotland as a panel member.

When it comes to racism, I never look for it, but I know it is there. If someone offends me, I tend not to see it as racism, unless it is blatantly obvious, like name calling in school. A pupil once took a picture of me from behind during one of my lessons and modified it to make me look fat and inserted a lot of junk food onto the picture before posting it on social media. The school dealt with this incident of racism appropriately by getting the pupil to apologise with a written note about the impact of his behaviour.

The worst racism I experienced happened about five years before I retired. A new head teacher at the school where I worked made me a scapegoat for his ineffectiveness in dealing with a pupil's behavioural issue across the whole school, he singled me out and implied that I was not fit to teach.

Despite being a chartered teacher with over 15 years of teaching experience without any complaints in all the years as a teacher, he put me through stage 1 of teacher competence procedures. He also tried to get me to take early retirement and for two years it was like a living "hell" – feeling humiliated, demoralised, stressed-out due to worries and these caused me many sleepless nights.

I performed all the appropriate tasks demanded satisfactorily just to prove to him that I was fit to teach. About a year later, the head teacher was removed from the school and demoted for incompetence. This experience is something I would not wish on anyone, but it has made me a stronger person.

In my experience, race relations have improved since I first came to the UK in the mid-70s. The worldwide Black Lives Matter protests in 2020 against racism have brought about positive changes in people's attitudes in society. Now in 2022, people generally are friendlier than in the past, there is more diversity in the media and more opportunities for black people in society.

We still have a long way to go to attain equality in a society where everyone, irrespective of race or skin colour is treated equally. All of us must continue to work together to eliminate racism and other forms of discrimination, prejudices and injustices caused by inequalities and to achieve this would help us all gain mutual respect.

Florence Baraza Menzies

MY LIFE IN KENYA AND SCOTLAND

Florence Baraza Menzies

MY LIFE IN KENYA AND SCOTLAND

My African name is Malala which means I was born at night. I was born in the rural western part of Kenya. My grandfather was a wealthy man, his shrewdness and arduous work earned him a position in a District Commissioner's office.

My grandfather discussed a bursary system he had heard of with my father telling him that he was to go to school. My father was an obedient son, so he did exactly as his father told him and he went to school for eight years.

After Primary 8 which had a school leaving certificate for education in those days, he was sent to learn brick making in a place called Nairobi which incidentally has grown to be a big city and the capital of Kenya today.

The girls, however, stayed at home. My grandfather decided that he was going to educate the girls in his family. In total, there were eight boys and three girls, his first granddaughter, I was the only girl who went to school.

When I was in Primary 6 my father passed away. He had always wanted me to continue with my schooling. By his passing, this meant my schooling was at an end. My mother took us and walked 45 km in the middle of the night to an orphanage run by the little sisters of St. Francis.

We found kindness and love there. The nuns registered us as orphans. Because my sister and I were older than the children in the orphanage, we were each given our room. My mother got a house at the mission for widows run by Guadeloupe Fathers.

Although our life and future were uncertain, we felt safe and protected by the nuns. The priests helped my mother and allowed her to visit us daily at the orphanage. The nuns organised and raised funds for my schooling throughout until I went to high school.

In high school, we had a visit by European women who came to our school to talk to us about their movement called the Grail. They explained to us that they were lay Catholic women who worked in communities as advisers who engaged in recruitment campaigns.

Later that week, I received a message to go to the office of the Grail administrator who informed me that an application had been made to Scotland on my behalf to train as a nurse. I was excited, on the other hand quite worried. I had never been away from the orphanage and was very naive to the outside world.

I was fearful to travel from Uganda to Scotland as it was my first time flying. When the plane touched down in Amsterdam and we had to change flights, I followed people who were connecting to various destinations. I made my connection to Scotland successfully; I was relieved that I was on my final leg to my destination.

At the airport, Auntie Rita was there waiting for me. She oversaw the Grail movement in Scotland, she advised that I should take it easy for a few more days to get used to the Scottish climate and get rid of the jetlag. She guided me in my early days in Scotland, she was an English lady, very kind and softly spoken. I stayed with Auntie Rita for three months before I started nursing training.

During this time, I had the opportunity to help the Bonnington Community Centre. It catered to children whose mothers went to work and the elderly people engaged in craft work. They were all looked after by the ladies of the Grail. Auntie Rita worked as a teacher.

On the first day at work, I discovered that I was the only black person there. When the children saw me, they ran to the furthest corner of the room. Their faces showed fright. After an introduction, we had an induction around the centre. The frightened children eventually got familiar with me.

They touched my hair, my skin, nails and even my teeth. By the end of three months, I started to get familiar with Scottish weather at this point.

Auntie Rita brought me some winter clothes. There was a large open fire in the living room that kept the place warm. I asked Rita why the dead trees had not been used as firewood. Auntie Rita laughed and explained to me it was autumn and trees shed their leaves and I would see a weather change. A white powder called snow in winter could make situations dangerous.

Another problem I had to deal with was understanding what people said. I had to listen carefully to the language. It was quite difficult to understand but as time passed, I began to know what they meant and understood the different ascents.

There was one occasion when someone addressed me as "hen" on the bus. I was quite upset as I thought the lady called me a chicken. When I got home, I informed Auntie Rita about the name calling, that someone called me a chicken on the bus. Auntie Rita burst out laughing because she explained that "hen" is the same as honey or sweetheart.

For those three months, I did not see Africans where I lived. I wondered whether there were Africans in Scotland. At the end of three months, a letter came from the South Edinburgh School of Nursing informing

me where to report for information related to our nursing training.

On the day of reporting, I found three other African students. One was from Ghana, two men and a girl from Rhodesia (now Zimbabwe), and a

Chinese girl called Cordelia, and me from Kenya. Information given to us was that we would go to six different hospitals during our three-year training. We were all divided up and sent to different hospitals.

I was happy that at least I had three African students training with me so that we could share our culture, talk about things that made us feel homesick and help each other out. For the first six months, I lived with Auntie Rita before I moved out to the nurses' home which was adjacent to the Hospital.

I will never forget my experiences of the second and third days in the ward. When we reported on duty. We gave patients breakfast; my duty was to go and feed an elderly lady who was sitting up in bed. I had a bowl of porridge in my hand as I approached her smiling. I said to her I was going to feed her. She looked at me and then shouted, "go wash your dirty hands." I was confused by the viciousness in her voice.

In my ignorance, I did not realise that she was being racist. I duly went and washed my hands to please her. When I came back, she told me my hands were still dirty, and with that, she knocked the bowl off and the porridge landed on her bedding. I could not laugh but it looked very funny.

Everyone knew the lady was racist and I did not know what racism was.

I was allocated to another patient who sat up in a chair and looked like she was asleep. So, I went to her and tried to wake her up, but she would not move. I told the duty staff nurse that she was unable to wake up. So, she came over to see if she could wake her up. She called me behind the curtains and told me that the patient was dead. I was given a cup of coffee to calm me down and half an hour later, I was back in the ward.

The next day, we made hot drinks for patients and cleaned their teeth later. Another student ran to the kitchen and said to me she was making the drinks and I should clean the patients' teeth. I was horrified at how I was going to take the teeth out of their mouths. She said I should ask them to remove them for me.

I went to the nearest patient and asked her to give me her teeth. She obliged and pulled out her teeth. I had nothing to put them in so I ran to the sluice and got a big bowl. I went round from patient to patient and asked them to put their teeth in the big bowl. When I had collected all the teeth I went into the sluice and ran water over them. I went and put the bowl of teeth in the fridge.

I worked on a late shift the following morning. Suddenly there was a big bang on my door. I was to report to the ward, everyone was quiet as the report briefing had taken place at the change of the shift. Duties had been allocated to the members of staff and it was breakfast time. The staff nurse asked me what I had done with the patients' teeth. Sheepishly and surely, I told them I did not know where to put them, so, I put them in the fridge.

Everyone laughed, I did not know what they were laughing at. The staff nurse and the Matron could not restrain themselves from telling me how stupid I was to do that. How were they going to know which teeth belonged to whom? I was lucky enough to have African friends whom I could share my experiences with.

Another thing that consumed me was, how to keep my culture alive. Life was moving so fast that I was getting worried that I would not remember my African way of life. I soon saw a stream of African women who came to visit Auntie Rita from other parts of Scotland, Europe, or even from Africa coming to stay and study. As time went by more Africans appeared on the streets of Edinburgh and the numbers started to grow.

This was a welcome change. For my third year, we were quite a big African Community in Edinburgh by then. The Edinburgh City Council created an International Club whereby all foreign students in Edinburgh would meet once a month together with the hosts to exchange news and views. The hosts befriended the foreign students and helped them to settle in or took them to their homes and showed them Scottish hospitality. I had three Scottish girlfriends and they took me to their homes.

At times, I found excuses not to go whenever I was invited. I was expected to go and wash their clothes. I could not understand how they would expect the visitor to do that. To them, it was great fun but later, I realised this was another form of racial abuse. My other two girlfriends behaved the same way. Never off duty at Christmas, Easter and public holidays. Patient allocation was the same. A patient gave me the name Tulip, he said it was his favourite flower and it comes in all colours.

After I qualified as RGN I went on to do Midwifery in England as I did not want to go home straight away. I went home after I qualified as a midwife RM. I was employed at the famous Nairobi Hospital, which was originally for Europeans only, but now it is for whoever can afford it, so most of the patients are politicians and extraordinarily rich businessmen/women.

I met my husband for the second time in Nairobi having met him for the first time in Scotland in 1972.

He came home from Tanzania where he was training Africans to be Lab Technicians. I was a second-year student nurse. After two months of meeting, he left again for Africa. This time to Kenya, where he worked in the veterinary laboratories to produce vaccines for the animals. We dated for a bit, got married the following year and returned to the UK together in 1975. We had three children, two in Aberdeen, one in Kenya, and we lived in Edinburgh.

My other passion, the Scottish Pipes and the African drums complemented each other quite well. My band was now complete but there was no name. The group name was a combination of Africa and Caledonia to give the name AFRIDONIA. We performed in many Edinburgh festivals, in fact getting 4-star and 5-star performances. We had the opportunity to go to Singapore to perform during their Arts Festival.

I restarted my storytelling once more in schools, charity organisations, and in old people's homes. I took part in Edinburgh festival storytelling and this was successful. I told stories in the Botanic Gardens building and the Lyceum. It was hard work, but it was rewarding and I enjoyed it. Looking back, I feel privileged that Scotland allowed me to bring a little bit of Africa to her shores.

To educate and share with her people what Africa and her people represent. I love Scotland, especially Edinburgh which kept calling me back no matter where I was. Here is where my life and love are centred, around my children and grandchildren. This is the only other place I want to be apart from Kenya, my country of birth.

Maltee Beeharee Seeruttun

NURSING BECAME A CAREER

Maltee Beeharee Seeruttun

NURSING BECAME A CAREER

I started my journey to the UK in September 1971. I was inspired by one of my aunties who came to London in the 1960s to further her education in teaching. She encouraged me to persue my dreams and develop my education to further my career. In September 1971, I left Mauritius which was a long and exhausting trip and arrived at London Heathrow to join my husband who was studying in Glasgow.

I stayed with his family for 2 weeks explored London and visited all the famous attractions. London was full of multicultural people working in shops, public transport and post offices. I thought London was a beautiful city indeed. After 2 weeks we travelled by train to Glasgow Central.

It was a shock to my system to see the difference in culture, atmosphere and most of all the weather. I remember people walking in long black jackets with their hoods up, Glasgow was very cold, dark and dirty which was the complete opposite of London.

On my first night in Glasgow, we stayed with my husband's friend in the Maryhill area. His wife was Irish and could not make a word she was saying, my husband, had to repeat after her. I remember the toilet being outside on the landing, the toilet roll was made from newspaper cuttings.

We rented a flat in Glasgow city centre, 93 Cambridge Street alongside a student who was studying engineering at Strathclyde University and came from Malawi. He gave me advice on where and how to survive in Glasgow, for example, to visit the library, understand how shops and banks worked. Staying in the city centre allowed me to explore the outer world.

My first hurdles were the language barrier compounded by local accent, slang, and dialects, the second biggest challenge was integration. I guess people were afraid of the unknown and took their time to speak to me as there were few people of colour in Glasgow. The weather was a big shock four seasons in a day rain, hailstorm, gale-force wind, black ice and snow which I thought was very dangerous, I still don't like the winter months.

I soon got used to wearing my long coat with a hood up too. I learned a lot from local people in the library. I wanted to study accountancy, but courses were too expensive so I had to rethink my career and see where I could earn and learn as it was a financial necessity. That was when I discovered the National Health Service was the way forward for me.

In October 1971, there was a gas explosion in Clarkson. I remember it so vividly as ambulances all over Scotland were dispatched to the scene. Twenty-two people lost their lives and hundreds were badly injured. It was like a horror movie and it gave me the motivation to work within the community.

In 1972, I started general nursing training at Glasgow Western and Gartnavel hospital groups. My classes were competitive but also very educational which inspired me to further expand my knowledge. It was an experience for me to do practical work in a hospital setting, as I had never once worked with the youth and it was tough going. I counted the days, however, I persevered and realised to pass my exams, I needed to focus on the assignment workload to achieve my qualification.

I was affected by race myopia, it hit me hard, as I had never been exposed to such a discriminatory environment. I was never prepared for an extreme culture clash. There was a variety of overseas nurses who felt the same degrees of prejudice and discrimination at work. I tried not to focus on racism it exists everywhere in the world.

I couldn't change it but can change my perspective and rise above it. One of the best parts of my training was the Ear, Nose and Throat Hospital. In a friendly hospital, I was welcomed and felt part of the community and bonded well with my team. My colleagues were supportive and that was how I managed to survive in a hospital environment.

One of my beautiful and funny experiences was the Glaswegian slang. I was so confused and uneasy that my colleagues used the term "hen", "luv", "pet" and "honey" when talking to me. I thought calling me pet was like calling me an animal or hen meaning I was running about like a headless chicken. Until I discovered the true meaning of the slang. I was so relieved and thought it was affectionate and a nice touch.

After graduating, I took a break and had my first baby son. At the time I was not given advice on maternity leave. There was a real challenge raising a family without a support network and then within six months, I had to re-apply for my job at the Western Infirmary, which I opted to do part-time, 20 hours of night duty because of family commitment. We bought our first flat in Mansfield, off Byres Road in the West End, which was within a walking distance of the hospital.

My husband and his friends started a business as property developers. I worked around shifts and childcare and brought up my son. We moved to Bishopbriggs, nearer to schools. Once my son started primary school, I had a lot of time, so I went back to college as a mature student and studied podiatry. My lecturers were supportive and advised me on what to do. Upon achieving my degree, I started my own business and named it Sheridan because it felt easy for people to pronounce and relate to.

Once I had my business up and running, I carried on working part-time for 18 hours a week at Stobhill Hospital while expecting my second baby. I passed my driving test and bought a car. I was blessed with a daughter in 1982. I went on full maternity leave. On my return, I worked in Glasgow Royal Infirmary as a senior staff nurse, it was a highly nit-picking working culture.

The distrust of overseas nurses and transferred nurses was obvious, I felt being monitored all the time. Racist comments were made openly, we were put down in front of patients and visitors. I was constantly criticised for one thing or another, I felt humiliated and helpless. I was disciplined for being overconfident and I was not the only nurse who felt like that.

I strived to maintain a high level of professionalism regardless of their attitude, thankfully it was rare, most of the time I found lovely, supportive patients full of gratitude for my hard work. Overcoming the challenges was my utmost achievement and a reward for me. Reflecting on my years in Scotland, I believe I had given my very best.

Throughout my life in Scotland, I have experienced and suffered the effects of negative psychological well-being. People say or do one thing that hurts even if they don't mean to. When I take a step back to access the situation logically rather than emotionally, then, there is not as bad as one would think. Life is what you make of it and having faith in oneself makes things possible. It's a beautiful world with nice people. I retired from NHS in 2017.

I am a member of the Glasgow swimming club. I remember many years ago people asked me why a person like me, an Asian was able to wear a swimming costume. I had to explain my culture and background were no different from anybody else. People are ignorant, at the end of the day we are all human beings we should learn to respect different cultures.

I met Dr Harriette Campbell in Unison meetings we became good friends. She introduced me to ACES and SOPA and I attended many meetings in Edinburgh. We were invited to join the Scottish Women's Convention celebrating women in Scotland on International Women's Day at the house of parliament where I met the first minister and many MPs.

I come from a middle-class family, I have five brothers and 3 sisters. My parents were entrepreneurs. I grew up learning a lot about business. Parenthood has been the most incredible element of my life. I have a

son and a daughter both highly educated and doing well in their life married with 2 young sons and they are adorable. I was reading a story that had an old lady with a lot of laugh lines on her face, my grandsons James said grandma don't change your face when you are old.

My grandson Daniel said he is Grandma's favourite because there is more photograph of him on the wall. My daughter is an independent woman who still wants to pursue further studies to build her own business. I continued my business of podiatry and beauty. My husband is also retired but continues to work in his business.

Marie Blackie-Ferguson

GLASGOW BORN AND BRED
WITH A RICH MULTICULTURAL HERITAGE

Marie Blackie-Ferguson

GLASGOW BORN AND BRED
WITH A RICH MULTICULTURAL HERITAGE

I was born on 30th July 1957 in Rottenrow Hospital, Glasgow. I have one sibling, a sister called Zanya who is eleven years younger than me.

My parents were Verona Louise Ferguson and Kofi Samuel Asiedu. My mother, Verona came from St Mary, Jamaica and my father was from Ghana which used to be known as the Gold Coast until independence on 6th March 1957.

Both my father and mother came from very large families. My maternal grandparents, Stanley and Doris Ferguson owned a large farm about fifty miles outside Kingston. My grandfather worked the land and did a bit of mining as well as some work for the local council. Together my grandparents raised eleven children.

My mother was the second oldest in the family, and already had a teacher training certificate from her studies in Jamaica, but instead of teaching decided to follow a nursing career. In 1955 she travelled to the UK as one of the "Windrush generations", those travelling to the UK between 1948 and 1975 from Caribbean countries on the Windrush ship to the UK to work.

I could never understand why my mother ended up in Scotland, but rumour had it that a young naval officer she met on board managed to convince her that Scotland would be a better place for her, so she decided to make her way further to the north.

When I was older, she told me Glasgow was a bit of a shock as she had expected to find purple heather and men in kilts, but Glasgow was dingy, smoke-filled and it never stopped raining. There was a lot of poverty in the city at that time too as the UK was recovering from the effects of the Second World War.

Nevertheless, she settled down to her studies and was housed along with other trainee nurses in a hostel owned by the Western Infirmary in Glasgow. She met my father about a year after arriving in Glasgow, which was an absolute miracle as nurses were ruled over with an iron fist, and socialising was frowned upon.

My mother trained to become a State Registered Nurse (SRN), rather than a State Enrolled Nurse (SEN) which had a shorter training period, but often relegated these nurses to more menial tasks.

Most immigrant nurses found it difficult to get past the SEN stage due to racial prejudice and discrimination, but my mother managed despite these obstacles and made friends with other young nurses from the Caribbean, Jamaica, St Vincent, Lucia, Trinidad, and many other islands.

Many of these nurses settled down and married in Glasgow, and their descendants are still in the UK today. There were fewer nurses from Africa, but as time went on the numbers increased.

My mother met my father at a nurses' dance organised for international students at Glasgow University by a rather upper-middle-class lady called Margaret Stuart, who became my godmother. My father was very proud of the fact that he came from Ghana.

My parents married in Lansdowne Parish Church, Great Western Road, Glasgow and almost immediately my mother found she was pregnant. My mother was still a student and apart from this in the 1950s once a woman got married she was usually expected to give up her career and become a housewife. The profession was seen as one for young, single women.

With no extended family or relatives around, childcare was difficult, so it was quite common for African students to arrange for their children to be temporarily fostered whilst they completed their studies.

They would place adverts in newspapers, shop windows, or magazines for suitable foster families. In my case, an advert was placed in "Nursery World" for a "nice family to look after a coloured baby". This was the term used at the time, and no one found it offensive and the word "black" was considered rather impolite. My parents managed to find a young Scottish couple, Betty and John McGuckion who had a daughter called Margaret who was about 8 years old.

Betty would never let me call her "mummy" since I already had one. We lived in a little council flat in Cranhill in the East End of Glasgow. We had a tiny black and white television set which they must have bought in 1953 to watch the coronation of the young Queen Elizabeth. We would sit around the TV in the evenings watching old films from the 40s, but our favourite program was the London Palladium Show.

One evening Shirley Bassey made a rare appearance, and Betty pointed at the screen saying, "that's your mummy". I was only about 4 years old and it was the only way they knew how to introduce me to the concept of multiculturalism. When I eventually met my mother again, I thought she did look a bit like Shirley Bassey, with her beehive hairstyle and elegant sense of style.

I got to know my parents when I turned five. The years I spent in Cranhill with Betty and John were happy ones. I was just one of the family, and despite the curious looks when I was taken out in my pram, it was a normal life. I had lots of Scottish aunties and uncles from the large McGuckion extended family.

Someone always seemed to be emigrating to Australia or Canada, and whenever this happened aunties, uncles, cousins and nephews all got together to give them a good send-off. Dozens of us would crowd into our tiny front rooms to sing or talk, recording our voices on tape to give them something to remember us by. Everyone would get quite emotional, crying into their beer and giving us the children sweets.

My birth parents visited as often as they could whilst I was with Betty and John, but I was too young to remember much. I did have recollections of my father showing Betty how to comb my hair. On one of his visits, I asked Betty where he was going. She told me he was going home.

She laughed when I asked whether he was going home to Ghana and reassured me that home was somewhere in the West End of Glasgow where the posh people lived. My father always seemed to be in a hurry. He cut quite a dash whenever he turned up at Lamlash Crescent, with his sleek well-groomed hair – and he always wore a suit.

My father had arrived in the UK to study Business Management at Glasgow University. His eldest brother called Kwame was a businessman and owned stores in Accra known as Asiedu Bros. His elder brother, Uncle Emmanuel, expected my father to return to Ghana to help run the business once he graduated.

Unfortunately, my father had his own plans. Despite the 1950s, the UK being desperate for workers from the British Colonies and

Commonwealth countries, prejudice was rife. It wasn't uncommon to see the sign "No Blacks, No Irish and No Dogs" outside lodging houses and rental properties.

If you had the money, you could buy your property instead of renting. My father scraped together all the money he had and bought a house in the west end of Glasgow. It was slightly dilapidated, but the main part of the house had seven bedrooms and the basement had a further three rooms and a bathroom and kitchen.

It was in a very desirable part of town, just off Byres Road and best of all he'd been able to avoid discrimination by becoming a landlord himself and renting to fellow students. 54 Cecil Street was to become our home for the next thirty years and formed the basis of all my childhood memories.

My parents knew I was happy with Betty and John, but now they were comfortable, despite the extortionate fees and planned to send me to the prestigious Laurel Bank for Girls which was across the road from us. We were spoilt for choice of good schools, and since I had already been enrolled at Dowanhill Primary, I stayed there where I was the only black child.

It was 1962, and I can remember my mother taking me there on my first day. We were late and she had on high heels, but we still managed to run! I loved school from the very first day and made friends immediately. My best friend was a little girl called Ella and we stayed friends for the next 20 years. I also had a boyfriend, a boy called Edward who was also six years old, had a mop of almost white blond hair and wore glasses. He would spoil me by taking me to the corner shop at lunchtime and spending twopence on sweets for me. I was heartbroken when his family moved and he went to a new school.

I was always happy at school and went to Brownies and Sunday school, but things were never right at home. I never saw much of my father as over the years he had completed his studies, studied French, German, and Russian and was working as an Interpreter at the United Nations in Geneva on six-month contracts. As a nurse, my mother worked on night shifts, but we had a cousin called Lydia from Ghana living with us, who was only 18 but was able to keep an eye on me since I was only 9 years old.

I also had a tutor who lodged with us and taught me arithmetic, which I was bad at. I was more artistic and I wanted to be an artist. Mr Gordon was a young man who looked like a monk. He was paid to take me to museums at the weekend, followed by an ice cream or lunch. Once a week I had violin lessons from Mr Secchi, an old Italian gentleman who lived a few doors away from us.

My mother was a keen pianist, she spent most of her free time playing the piano. She had a lot of friends, mostly from the Caribbean. She'd invite them round to the house and the smell of singed hair from the hot comb would often greet me on my return from school. That and the smell of nail varnish.

My mother was obsessed with looking after her hands so kept her hands beautifully manicured and employed a cleaner to scrub, clean and iron our bed linen for us and for the tenants in the house their washing was put into a big black trunk with the words "Clydesdale Cleaning" on it and were then picked up and returned all washed and crisply ironed.

Our family name was actually "Asiedu" but no one could pronounce it properly, including my mother and the cleaner as they were not Ghanaians. Everyone including the neighbours called my mother "Mrs Assaytoo". In those days supermarkets didn't exist so there was an endless round of trips to the butchers, fishmongers, greengrocer bakers and more. "Good morning, Mrs Assaytoo", was the familiar greeting I heard as a child when we were out shopping.

My father's Geneva contract with the UN ended and he acquired several more properties and thought of opening a café in Partick, on Merkland Street where Morrisons Supermarket is situated now. He was going to call it "The Kofi Cup". He had also opened a bed and breakfast on Ashley

Street in Charing Cross and asked my foster parents, Betty and John, to help him run it. They readily agreed and I was delighted as they would be within walking distance of us, which was better than taking a long journey to the East End.

The Kofi Cup café was run by Mrs Gertrude Constance, a long-time family friend. She had come over from St Vincent back in the late 1950s or early 60s. She was a widow with five children. They all lived on Kersland Street and were one of the few Caribbean families in the neighbourhood. Like us, they had a good family network as her sister and her children lived in the West End too.

By now my mother had given birth to my sister, Zanya, and wanted to visit Jamaica and show them the new baby who was only a few months old. Looking back now, I think my mother was probably very homesick, disillusioned at not being able to pursue her career in medicine and possibly suffering from postnatal depression. In any event, once back in Jamaica she decided to pursue her career as a Senior Health Nurse and did not return to Glasgow for twenty years.

I stayed here with my father, and after leaving school studied for a couple of Higher National Diploma (HND) courses in Business Administration, French and German. I met a charming Nigerian man in Glasgow in 1976. I was only 19, but a few years later we got married and went to live in Nigeria. Life in Lagos was so different from Glasgow, but we were comfortable.

I found being a British expatriate in Nigeria offered many opportunities there, I made friends with women from all over the world and I learned so much about Nigerian culture. My new in-laws were kind, but I really couldn't see myself settling for life there. I missed Scotland and my family and came back with my son and daughter in 1988.

Once I got back, it was easy to pick up where I had left off. I'd been coming back every year with the children anyway, so it didn't feel as if I had cut ties altogether with my homeland. Schools for the children weren't a problem, as they just went to the same ones I went to.

A few years after my return, I went back to university and got a degree in Information Management & Business in 1994. In 1996 I started working in Telecommunications as a Sales & Marketing Coordinator. Within a few years, I was an Acquisitions Surveyor/Engineer for a well-known Glasgow organisation. Looking back, I'm quite proud of the decision I made and what I achieved.

It's such a male-dominated field, with 87% male and 13% female and I was the only black female surveyor in the whole of Scotland. One of a handful working in the field in the entire UK. I never saw this as strange or thought of myself as different as I seem to have always worked in companies where I was the only woman.

I enjoyed my job. One of the things that amused me was turning up on-site and seeing half a dozen engineers waiting for the surveyor. I'd put my hard hat on and asked, right, are we all ready to go? By signalling, we can start the day's work! It's such a professional field and everyone works as a team to get the job done. I never met anyone who had a problem taking orders from a female.

I would recommend engineering to any woman. The men I worked with were all on high salaries with top-of-the-range company cars. Once I started working with them, they gave me tips on how to negotiate for a wage rise or a better car. "Don't bother telling your manager you love your job", one of my senior colleagues up in Aberdeen told me. "Just tell him you deserve a pay rise and that's it".

I sometimes missed working with other females, but most of the time the buzz of the job, the financial rewards and seeing a project through to completion made up for everything. More women should look into engineering, I think. There are so many openings for them.

I left telecommunications in 2004 to set up my own marketing business which I ran for a few years as I couldn't see myself driving all over the British countryside and being 30 metres up in a cherry picker in my 50s as a surveyor. I had always enjoyed working with people and with a qualification in Psychology, I took a year out of communications to retrain as a Clinical Hypnotherapist and Counsellor. It was the best thing I have ever done, up until the lockdown in 2020 I ran a successful therapy business and over the years treated hundreds of patients.

After the lockdown, I never reopened. Back in 2012, I was diagnosed with breast cancer. This was successfully treated only to come back in 2017 as Stage 4 breast cancer which is treatable, but not curable. Holding down a full-time job or running a business with all the commitments it entails was too much difficult. However, now that my condition seems to be under control, who knows?

On a positive note, my mother loved her work and found her fellow Scottish nurses to be kind at heart, and she made many friends. She also had quite a comfortable life. She also didn't have to worry about childcare.

My mother gained a wealth of experience in many hospitals. Apart from working in the UK she also went to work in the West Indies where she became a highly qualified Health Nurse.

After her retirement in Glasgow in 1991, she continued to work for charitable organisations, including the Glasgow School for the Blind. Being a keen academic, she continued to study and in 2006 at the age of 77 was awarded her MSc from the University of Wales. Verona Louise Ferguson was laid to rest in Glasgow on 17th January 2017 at the age of 90 years old.

By the mid-1960s you could say they had made it. Life had been good to young Kofi. While still in his 30s my father had accumulated several properties in Glasgow, including a B & B, a café in Glasgow's Partick and an antique shop in the city's fashionable West End.

He was well able to provide for his wife whether she worked or not. The income from his properties provided him with financial freedom and by now had built up a network of friends and contacts within the Scottish and the immigrant community. He was also able to pursue his love of cars.

In the 1960s car ownership was not as common as it is now, but he managed to be the proud owner of a Citron and a Bentley, which unfortunately never seemed to get moving, but allowed my father many hours of pleasure tinkering about under the bonnet, to the amusement of our neighbours.

Hillhead was a good place to bring up children in those days, as Glasgow University was still being built so there was lots of space. Schools were good, and there was the option of the elite Laurel Bank School for Girls, which my father now toyed with the idea of sending me to despite the fees.

My father had a colourful life. He continued with his business ventures in Glasgow, got tired of accumulating real estate and returned to his native Ghana in the late 1990s. He passed away and was laid to rest 20 years ago in Accra, Ghana – West Africa.

Mary Osei-Oppong

FROM GHANA TO GLASGOW

Mary Osei-Oppong

FROM GHANA TO GLASGOW

I am going to tell you a little bit about my life in Glasgow.

I came to the UK in May 1982 from the Ashanti Region in Ghana, West Africa. I first arrived at London Heathrow Airport and spent one week in London and then came to Glasgow the following week by train.

My very first experience was getting used to wearing a long coat. It was May and summertime when most people in Glasgow were in summer clothes. The people I met thought the temperature was warm enough, but I felt cold. You can imagine, I came from a place with temperatures of above thirty degrees centigrade so when it's below twenty degrees, it was cold. The weather was my first adjustment.

I soon realised that it rained a lot in Glasgow. Then autumn came and I felt extremely cold for the first time in my life. I then discovered gas heaters with visible flames. To keep me warm, I used to sit close to the gas heater but soon got burnt and found decolourisation of skin on my legs. That was an eye-opener!

Then came getting used to the food, for example, potato-based foods. In the 80s there were not a lot of the so-called exotic fruits and vegetables available. I ate a lot of rice dinners, but not by choice. Eventually, I found Yeoman's mashed potato powder and a starch powder called Farina. It enabled me to start making a substitute Ghanaian meal called "fufu" and making typical Ghanaian (Asante) soup. It was a bit tricky, but it helped me enjoy dinners more in the early days.

Another challenge was the ability to communicate effectively - not that I couldn't speak English - it was the accent. It was difficult to start with, but I listened to the radio as well as watched TV and this helped me a lot to understand the different accents. It has to be said it was difficult for some of the people I met also to understand my accent as well.

I felt that Scotland was beautiful and most people were kind and helpful. I particularly liked the architecture and still do.

A big culture shock was to realise that some people in the UK slept rough. And the appetite for alcohol and the foul language spoken. The image held of the British in Ghana at that time was one of high esteem, so to find some people around town heavily drunk, some sleeping rough and members of the public swearing like troopers were all very shocking to me.

Also, the colour of clothes people wore at the time were mostly dark colours. In Ghana, people wore and still wear vibrant colours. So, looking for clothes to buy was a challenge, as I was fixed on bright colours, but I soon got used to that.

My biggest challenge has been integration. I went to places and expected to be accepted – just like Ghanaians accepted British there – but that was not the case. Some people did not want to come close to me. I suppose some people were and still are afraid of the unknown. In the early 80s, there were not a lot of Africans or Caribbeans in Scotland and among the other black people I met, most of them were students.

I lived in the West End of Glasgow, to be precise, West Princess Street, Saint George's Cross and after that Park Road next to Kelvinbridge Tube Station on Great Western Road for the first seven years.

When I first came to Glasgow, I got very homesick and still do from time to time. I missed my family the most, my mother, father and siblings. I also missed the food, culture, people, pleasantness, weather, outdoor festivities around Christmas time, Easter time and the feeling of belonging.

To continue my education, I embarked on several courses to refresh my education including Food Handling and Hygiene, Accounting and Computing Applications. I then studied for a Higher National Diploma in Computing and Business Administration. I studied for a degree in Computing and Business Administration.

I went on to a teacher training college to gain Postgraduate Certification in Education (Secondary).

I specialised in Computing Science and Business Education/Studies as my two main teaching subjects and Religious Education as a generalist. I achieved all this in one year and later qualified as a Chartered Teacher.

My biggest achievements have been my three children, working hard with commitment and dedication and being able to teach in Scotland for twenty two years. In my role as a classroom teacher, I campaigned tirelessly for equality in education and society, always aiming to integrate and add value to society.

In July 2020, I wrote a book called "For The Love of Teaching; The Anti-Racist Battlefield in Education. It was published in October and launched on 21st November 2020. The Educational Institute of Scotland (EIS) featured my book in their Scottish Educational Journal on 10th December 2020 and the European Trade Union Committee for Education also featured my book in the #SupportTeachersForInclusion campaign on 18th December 2020.

I've had some success with the message my book carries, the readership includes, teachers, lecturers, parents, nurses, activists, lawmakers, social

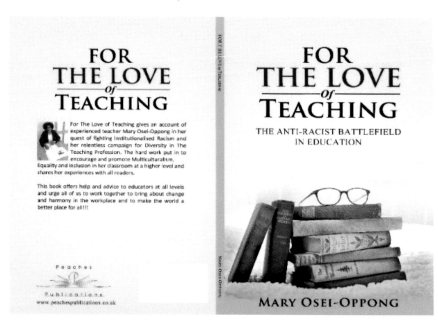

care staff and many more. My book has been used as a resource for development training in educational settings. It has been purchased all over the world! It is available on Amazon and here is the purchasing link: amzn.to/2Km5dD4

I had made an impactful contribution to Scottish Education and at the back of my book's publication, I took the plunge to engage in public speaking to enable people affected by inequalities to transform their own lives.

I am the current chairperson of the African Caribbean Women Association (ACWA) Scotland, ex-general secretary of the Ghana Welfare Association Glasgow, a founding member and an executive member of the Ghana Diaspora Scotland Committee.

A founding member and an executive member of the African and Caribbean Elders in Scotland, a Board Member of the West of Scotland Regional Equality Council (WSREC) and a Human Rights campaigner. I take my social responsibilities seriously and I have worked hard to make a difference in many communities across Scotland.

Riccarda Wanjiru

SCOTLAND IS MY HOME

Riccarda Wanjiru

SCOTLAND IS MY HOME

I came to Scotland to visit a friend. I wanted to go to Edinburgh because we used to have the Scottish church in Kenya, we called it PCEA back home, the Presbyterian Church of East Africa, like the Church of Scotland. I wanted to travel to see the place where the church originated.

When I arrived in Scotland, I found the Scottish people friendlier than the English, because I had stayed previously for some time in Oxford. I found it easier to relate to the Scottish because whenever I was up and about, I greeted strangers and they responded to me.

After a couple of weeks, I felt the differences. In Africa, you say: 'hello' to everyone even though you don't know them, but you expect friendliness from people. But in England, if you say 'hello' to someone, you are met with silence, I wondered why people didn't respond. I found out that most people were friendlier in Scotland.

I came to the UK in the year 2005 from Kenya and came to Scotland towards the end of the year 2006. I was here on a visit earlier in that year, around January and stayed for a few months. I stayed in Oxford for almost two years and wished to study at college. When I arrived in the United Kingdom, I was not very sure I wanted to stay because I came in November and it was very cold, but circumstances made me stay.

Continuing my education was my desire when I was in Kenya, I wanted to study aromatherapy, so when I came to Oxford, I tried to find out how to enroll in a college, but somehow it didn't work out.

When I moved to Scotland, Cardonald College Glasgow offered me a place on their aromatherapy course. I was not able to join the course at the first offer, because I was unwell. I enrolled in the course in the following academic session. It was quite an interesting experience. I had a good academic performance in the theory part of the course, but not in the practical part.

The main aspect of the practical part was carried out most times while on our feet, unfortunately, I developed arthritis which made it difficult for me to be in a standing position for a long time as the practical course required. I dropped out of college due to my inability to be on my feet for a good length of time as my body was not able to take it.

Before my arrival in the country, I had contact with many British people. Some teachers in the school I attended were from Britain and Ireland. I assumed everyone was accepting. I was shocked to find out about the discrimination that existed in the UK.

It was a culture shock as everything I knew was different from what I was confronted with, for example, the cold temperatures. In Kenya, my country of birth, it's quite warm in November. I was not prepared for the weather on my arrival in the UK, I was dressed in warm-weather clothing and that was the first time I wore a pair of trousers.

Also, I was shocked by some other things I saw. I couldn't believe that there could be beggars and people struggling in the UK. When I visited the Church I was warmly received by the church. Although I am not a Church of Scotland member, I used to attend Church of Scotland and I was warmly received. When I moved to Royston, Charles Street, I started attending the Catholic Church called Saint Roch's. The congregation and priest were all very kind and made us all feel very welcome. I was born and brought up as a Catholic, but now a Pentecost member.

On my first trip to Scotland, I went to Edinburgh with my friend for two days. We boarded a tour bus in Edinburgh and stayed at a bed and breakfast for the night and returned to Glasgow the following evening. It was summertime, the weather was good and we enjoyed the trip.

The long summer daylight was a shock, you know where I come from, we don't change the clock. I couldn't figure out why that was the case. I was more in shock by the experience of darkness at 4:00pm. The language was another challenge for me to settle into the Scottish community. However, I was able to find my way around it and soon got to understand the different accents.

There were black people in the community when I arrived, but not as many as at the present time. A good number of Africans and Caribbeans are now in Scotland more than when I arrived. This makes me feel better. I now find more black people on the buses, in the streets and in the workplaces. There were only two black people where I used to work and by the time I was leaving the job, there were more than two black people.

I had challenges with the food as well. These days there are more African shops where you can buy African foods that I am used to. Then, it was only one African shop in the city – on Great Western Road, Solly's.

I claimed asylum and later received training in social care and now work as a Carer. I have achieved Level 3 Scottish Vocational Qualification (SVQ 3) in Care and now, I want to study journalism. I felt homesick at times, too, and as a result, I thought what I was going through may not be worth the trouble. I left my family in Kenya, I have got my elderly parents to think of and I felt I had to push on for the sake of my family. I didn't intend to stay for long when I first came to the UK but here I am, it's well with me and my trips to Kenya now are on visits.

Back in Kenya, I worked in a bank, but now find my care job more satisfying to me than working in a bank. I wouldn't go back to a banking job. I do miss Kenya's weather, the food, and my school friends. I have missed out on a lot of things, like family occasions but for events that are planned, I could make time to go home but can't make all of them because it's expensive.

I am a first child and that comes with responsibilities. It makes me feel like a parent to my younger siblings. I am happy because I have been able to put the children through school. The children including my younger brothers are now settled. This gives me a lot of satisfaction anyway.

Living in Scotland has given me so much and I now have a network of friends. I have got friends from all over the world. I am quite happy and lucky.

Also, I am grateful to Dr Harriette Campbell, who introduced me to the African Caribbean Women Association (ACWA) Scotland. We met at work. We were the only two black people in this workplace, and we got talking and since then we've stayed in touch.

I am grateful we've got African and Caribbean Elders in Scotland (ACES), I am very happy because I have met people from all over Africa and the Caribbean and it feels like we are all one big family!

I had Coronavirus, and after that, I have become forgetful. They say it's brain fog, I hope it goes away but overall, I am in good health, that is the most important aspect in life.

Osman Lamin Sidique

MY JOURNEY IN LIFE AND MY FAMILY

Osman Lamin Sidique

MY JOURNEY IN LIFE AND MY FAMILY

Early in Sierra Leone (1977 – 1982 then 1992), after working hard to complete the academic process, one is always hopeful for a job. So you can start to reap the fruit of your labour.

In my case, I was rather lucky to secure a job quickly as an accountant for a new construction company as one of the recruits. It was challenging as structures and processes needed to be put in place to help the company grow.

After gaining some experience, I left and joined my father who was an entrepreneur and with the determination to help my father expand his business was short-lived because that year war broke out in Sierra Leone.

During the eleven years of civil war, most people fled to Guinea including my family. While in Guinea, I was lucky enough to secure a position with the United Nations. I engaged in buying and selling in Guinea before the United Nations appointment,

Still working with the United Nations and at this time in Kosovo. My family then returned to Sierra Leone, Freetown. During my first year in Kosovo, my wife and our family sought asylum in the UK and after some initial challenges, they were granted British Citizenship.

I visited my family in the UK from time to time while still working with the United Nations and during this time my daughter was born in 2004 in Glasgow, Scotland. I was later sent to work in Liberia where and after some time, I retired and joined my family in the UK in 2008.

The same year just after joining my family in the UK, my father died in Sierra Leone. My father's death made me return to Sierra Leone for his funeral. During my time in Sierra Leone, I worked with my cousin to become a hotel business partner.

This partnership was short-lived as the business was mysteriously burnt to the ground. I made a decision to join my family in the UK for good. Unfortunately, just after my arrival, I fell ill and after the treatment, I needed time to recuperate and it took a while for me to heal.

I felt better at this point and took a voluntary consultancy work with Kelvin College and Rosemount life-long learning. After working with the college for some time, a vacancy for a Gallery assistant for Black Minority Ethnic was advertised, I discussed it with my line manager and he recommended that I apply and I did exactly that and secured the position. This was full-time but temporary. I then looked for a permanent position and I was made permanent but part-time.

I used to accompany my wife to the African Caribbean Women Association (ACWA) Scotland meetings and met some of the members and in due course, I was invited to be a founding member of the African and Caribbean Elders in Scotland (ACES).

I am a news freak, listening to good music especially old-time favourites and a lot of walking are a few of my hobbies. Walking goes along with my sports activities. Thankfully at the moment, I work part-time at a sports establishment, as such availed the opportunity to engage in other sports like badminton and table tennis.

I am proud enough to describe my wife as one of the best cooks I have ever known. Invariably she cooks practically most of the best dishes one

can imagine with a particular focus on our local dishes from Sierra Leone. My wife is also the proud mother of all my seven children. A dedicated and devoted Mum. Among my children, we have three living with us in Glasgow, two of them born in Glasgow. The rest are in the US and Sierra Leone respectively.

My family attends the Bishopbriggs Community Church. We always consider the Church members as our family with a Pastor whom we are very close to I recall when I was diagnosed with bowel cancer about four years ago, our Pastor was never tired of paying us visits with very fervent prayers. I thank the Lord for letting me pass through that ordeal. Presently I had been officially declared cancer free.

Another memorable event was the renewal of our vows in 2018 almost coinciding immediately after my bowel cancer surgery. The ceremony was officiated by the Bishopbriggs Community Church led by our soul mate Pastor. A very memorable occasion backed by some friends around Glasgow gracing the occasion at the reception at Sight Hill Hub.

Presently I am doing part-time work at Kelvinhall. I have been working there for a little over three years now. Unfortunately, I happen to be the only African in that sporting establishment as an Activity Assistant. There was an incident just after my first year with them.

A colleague of mine barred the door of our supervisor's office preventing me from entering but allowing other Scottish folks to enter the office. But I just ignored him and walked into the office. I later discovered that he has been hostile to a couple of Africans who had been there before me. To date, this member of staff and I are poles apart.

As I have already mentioned being a loner can be painful at times. Supervisors and other colleagues can form a habit of ganging up like "Mafia". But it doesn't bother me at all. I pray that the Lord opens another door, like becoming successful in developing my charity organisation to a level where I no longer work for anyone but rather help people in need. Life goes on in Scotland and the struggle continues!

In conclusion, I want to thank the Almighty God for keeping my family neatly together in Glasgow. One would say destined to live in the Rosemount/Springburn neighbourhood all these years. It has been a richly rewarding experience living away from an African home to settle with another special home here in Scotland.

Ruth McCalla

HOME IS WHERE MY HEART IS

Ruth McCalla

HOME IS WHERE MY HEART IS

It was always on my bucket list to come to Scotland, but not in the way it happened. I first arrived in Ireland, lived in Ireland and got married there. My husband who is Scottish decided to return home to Scotland. That was how I came to Scotland.

I arrived in Scotland in 2016 and by 2018 we realised things were not working out between my husband and me, so we went our separate ways with a lot of affrays. But one of the things I vividly remember about this experience is how quickly I was able to bounce back and got a lot of things sorted out and moved on.

The Glasgow City Council's slogan "People Make Glasgow" became true and alive in my breakdown experience, because within months of our separation and going through its personal trauma, I was able to put my foot down and say: well this is where I belong and I'm staying.

There are so many similarities between Glasgow, Scotland as a nation and Jamaica. The networks within the Scottish communities made it even easier for me because this one knows that one and that one knows the other one, before I knew it, I was head-deep into so many projects.

I arrived first in Ireland in 2002 and I made Ireland my home. You make do with what you have until you can make a change, but the change that came was unexpected and at times that's how life happens.

In life, as time passes by, changes happen that you have not planned for and these changes could be the most effective; the best changes or experiences that I needed to divert the course of my life to be who I wanted to be and the way forward.

Within a year of being in Glasgow, I became a human rights activist and an advocate for domestic abuse survivors. I have sat on a few boards and done things that I never thought I could do – advocate for people's rights to ensure that justice is met and hold people to account. So, in the last six years, I have accomplished more than ever before.

I think it is best not to set high expectations that are not realistic because when I have expectations and they are not achieved, I am met with a sense of disappointment, which can easily turn into mental ill-health issues. I had an open mind coming to Scotland because I was an avid reader at that time and read about Scotland. Also, I had a Scottish friend and we worked in the same hospital, so, I had some knowledge about Scotland before I dreamt of coming to Scotland.

My initial impression of Scotland was: hmm, this is not different from Ireland and it is not different from Jamaica. The difference was that there were so many different accents, many different food types and there were many new things to learn and a lot of opportunities to further my education, I received support and encouragement to learn as much as possible and grabbed the chances that were offered to me.

So, I assessed the opportunities and then the discussions started, I even surprised myself because what I learned at university and on the job back in Jamaica came in handy and I was able to put it into practice, I did not realise my true potential until it was pulled out of me.

There were a few culture shocks on my path in Scotland, especially when it came to politics, football, family and behaviours. Depends on the football team you support; I was careful not to end up on the wrong side of the fence. I was careful where I went and what I said in particular about football clubs and fans.

Also, I learned very quickly in relation to party politics. I relied on my skill set gained through being a parent, teacher and my knowledge in public relations to navigate and chart through the waters instead of ruffling feathers and causing animosity.

I lived in the Central Belt of Scotland when I first came here in a little village. I was the only black person there, until months after, I met another black person who lived a little further away from me.

I went to places like Livingston, Edinburgh, or Glasgow, it felt like home as I saw a lot of black people and a lot of Asian and Minority Ethnic people as well. On the news channels and going to hospitals, I saw a lot of nurses, carers and doctors, this made me aware of the diversity that exists in the workplaces in Scotland.

When I first came to live in Glasgow in 2018, I felt it was diverse because by joining various support groups, I realised that there were a lot of black people from different ethnic minority groups. Then, I started going out and about and getting more involved and meeting more from all walks of life.

I asked myself, so where were they hiding? They were where they have always been, I said, it's just that I wasn't going to those places. I met Harriette Campbell in 2019 at the Scottish Parliament. That's when my work with the African Caribbean Women Association (ACWA) Scotland started.

I was so busy when I was first introduced to ACWA, I was up and down, then I fell ill and was admitted to the hospital. When I was discharged from the hospital, I remember the secretary, Jamilah Hassan, calling me to find out if I still wanted to be a part of the ACWA group. At that stage, I was recuperating. I felt it was too much, so I said no! I'm glad that Jamilah was persistent and told me to think about it and that she will call back later.

I remember my first ACWA meeting, I still couldn't see properly, it was December 2019 when I went to one of ACWA's in-person meetings and that was an experience I haven't looked back since. That showed me that there were black people around who cared. There was a feeling of sisterly love and people who were not afraid to say what I needed to do with love, support and encouragement.

I remember Margaret Addo, she was one of the few who gave me a call and asked how my recovery was going. So, I always looked forward to her calls, and it showed that the old matriarchal care was still alive. I remember if it wasn't Margaret Addo calling me, it was Harriette Campbell calling me, to find out how I was doing. For example, they would ask, did you take your medication? When is your next doctor's appointment? Can you manage? If I even wanted to back out of ACWA, what these women did in that sense was to pull me into the group more.

I had already met Margaret Lance elsewhere before I came to ACWA. Margaret would see me outside ACWA and ask 'how are you doing my sister and how are you feeling now? That made a big difference. Jamilah would call me do you need anything? That made a difference because I rest assured that they were there for me in my time of need.

I think because I have always said that - home is where the heart is, I think I'm a bit strange in the sense that the things that I can't change, I find an alternative way to it, that's how I deal with homesickness. And I said that if I am not able to go home to Jamaica, then I'm going to make my home in Glasgow feel like Jamaica. And that's exactly what I have done.

I joined Migrants Organising for Rights and Empowerment (MORE) and the LGBT Health and Wellbeing, where I volunteer and support people who are coming from different continents and who are seeking to come out. I also support asylum seekers and refugees. Also, I am a member of the African and Caribbean Elders in Scotland and joined in 2020.

So, it's one thing to have support but it's another thing to give support. You can't give what you don't have. It feels great for me to be able to still give back to my community.

I miss Jamaican food because normally in Jamaica you could go outside and cut your banana fresh from the tree in the backyard. You could get fresh yams and there is a variety of yams. You could get breadfruit, roast, steam, boil, or you can even add it to your soup. I miss the aroma of Saturday cooking in the community. You smell the soup cooking on a Saturday, and you can say: great, my neighbours are cooking peas soup or that smells like beef soup.

I miss Sundays having my neighbours coming in, or me going to theirs and having dinner with them. At Christmas time, everybody's door is open. People don't make a religion or anything like that come between neighbours. Then coming to Scotland and realised I have to be politically correct, it's a learning process, because if we all did things the same way, life would be boring.

When I came to Scotland. It was my intention to become a resident in Scotland, but things in my personal life and my breakdown got in the way. I made sure that I sought the help of a friend and a few agencies to help me recover. I was able to get my life back on track and in 2019 I started looking for a job.

By October 2019, I was losing my sight and by the 30th of October, I was hospitalised and in a coma. When I came out of the coma, I was told that I was diabetic. And this could have been averted if my condition was taken seriously by the doctors. I kept saying to them: 'I'm losing my sight', there was nothing done other than constantly adding more tablets to the prescriptions I was on already.

When I look back it felt that the doctor showed how misogynistic he was, also, showed that racism was alive and well in the medical field. There I was in my vulnerable state and I kept asking myself even now: what was he trying to do? Was he trying to cause me harm? Or he was just simply racist?

I remember when I was discharged from the hospital and went back